In the Pocket

In the Pocket

Bryan Kromm

First Edition

Edited by J.L. Powers
Cover Design by Paul Scarlata

ISBN 979-8-9888687-0-5 (paperback)
ISBN 979-8-9888687-1-2 (ebook)

Published by Bryan Kromm

Dedicated to my soulmate, my family, my bosses, and the authors of the books who all inspired me to write.

I

Introduction to Story Three

How can you write a book in one minute? Write down one sentence. He was exercising his newly learned technique: *Kaizen*. Small steps for change, or improvements. He wanted to write a book. The task didn't seem too daunting, he had all the ideas in his head. The only thing left to do now was un-jumble the mess he had created in his mind. *Get your ideas out on paper so you can make sense of them,* he thought.

Thoughts were recurring impulses that required action to be satisfied. "Do something about them," he told himself. "You really have to work up the courage to 'do something'."

In the Pocket

His thoughts, at the moment, were ripe for the picking, and if he ever got around to harvesting them, he'd reap the rewards—only afterwards to find another tree, seeded, sprouted and ready to be tended. We enjoy the fruits of our labor, not realizing there will be another harvest. People walk through a city wishing to find open space, and people in open space wish for something to look at.

The world is funny if you open your eyes. For instance, he learned in *One Small Step Can Change Your Life: The Kaizen Way* by Robert Maurer to "ask small questions" to himself (55). The more you repeat the question, according to the book, the more curious your mind becomes in answering the question (60). "How can you write a book in one minute?"

You see, he woke up that morning to make his coffee; he boiled the water and poured it over the grinds, timing the brew for five minutes as he usually did to make sure it was made properly, and as he did so, his thoughts were at it again, unruly and growing wild. So, he thought he'd try this *Kaizen* thing out and write down a sentence. While he was working at this, the timer for his coffee was quietly counting down each minute out of sight, as his one sentence turned into five and he got up to pour his cup of coffee. The world *is* funny if you open your eyes.

Here's some more proof. He had this impulse to write a book, so he took the next logical step—find out how to write one. Amongst the common tips of internet professionals was a seemingly trivial one at the time—if you want to write a book, read one. So, using more wisdom from his internet experts, he compiled a list of the "greatest novellas of all time" and started to knock them off day by day, page by page. First was George Orwell's *Animal Farm*, then Steinbeck's *Of Mice And Men*. He worked his way through Salinger's *The Catcher In The Rye* and now was finishing Coelho's *The Alchemist*. Interestingly, these "trivial" readings began to shape his writing and form his ideas more clearly. Their relatively small shapes and sizes, and their immensely powerful messages, gave him courage. They were guiding him through his journey, and he could sense it. He always had that sense—like he was on to something. Just like the shepherd in *The Alchemist* following the omens in pursuit of his treasure, he too was listening to the signs of his life leading him to his purpose (Coehlo 31-32).

In the Pocket

More and more things were happening. For instance, he took a trip to the Yukon to celebrate the marriage of an old college roommate and planned a three-day hiking trip afterwards. Each mountain he climbed seemed unfathomable as he stared at it from afar. "I'm going to climb that?!" He laughed at the improbability. And it would have been improbable had he kept staring at it. Do something. One step, no matter how small. Over and over again looking up at the peak with wonder, exhaustion, and despair, he continued to chant his mantra softly to himself. "It's okay, just one more step." At times he dangerously lost his footing while looking upward and was reminded to keep his focus on each step. And at times when he focused too much on each step, he veered off course. This curiously reminded him of the story within *The Alchemist* of the boy who had to focus on the spoon of oil he carried, careful not to spill it, while exploring everything the world had to offer within the wise man's castle (33-35). Eventually, no matter how slow, labored, and small his steps were, and no matter how many breaks he took, he would summit. And after enjoying the quiet beauty of the top of the world, he would descend the same way he climbed. And after the descent, he would enjoy the safety of level ground and the view of the mountains from afar.

At the beginning of that same trip, he began Bronte's *Wuthering Heights*. Just as the family story started to unravel, and his attempts to put down the book became less and less, he mindlessly left the book on the plane. While perusing downtown Whitehorse the next day he came across a bookstore, and wandered in to search for a replacement. Instead, he found London's *The Call of the Wild* and *White Fang*, along with *The Urge: Our History of Addiction* by Carl Erik Fisher, which was a comparatively larger and more modern book than that of London's.

As he read Fisher's book, more of his own thoughts and ideas were understood:

> Some explanations frame addiction as a manifestation of "psychological inflexibility": attempts to manipulate and avoid negative thoughts and feelings by disappearing into addictive behaviors, including not just substance use but also worry, rumination, self-stimulation, and other forms of mindlessness. Those avoidant responses are a kind of self-

> medication, not in the sense that addiction
> is the superficial expression of a "deeper"
> problem, but rather that substance
> addictions are merely one variant of a
> universal feature: the way our human
> psychology sometimes reacts ineffectively
> to pain (Fisher 14-15).

Maurer posits in his book on *Kaizen* that there
is a fear of uncertainty innate in all of us (42-43).
It is a fear we avoid, but it is through overcoming
it that we thrive, and in life, uncertainty is
inevitable. Isn't that beautiful?

He pulled another excerpt from Fisher:

> There is also a psychological dislocation
> that can be just as toxic: being torn from
> culture and traditional spirituality, losing
> freedom and self-determination, and lack-
> ing opportunities for joy and self-
> expression. Even for those of us who are
> not suffering from such tangible depriva-
> tions today, we are just as vulnerable as
> our ancestors, if not more so, to the
> psychospiritual ones (Fisher 37).

He scribbled the passages feverishly as if the completion of his book depended on it. He knew enough about negative coping mechanisms through his degree in psychology, and through personal experience. He didn't scribble them for his own confirmation, what he wanted was to explain it to someone else. He wanted to provide a solution—a why, a how, and a what. How can every person no matter their ethnicity, race, color, creed, life experience, socioeconomic status, education level, age, sex, gender survive their suffering? It is because it is what life intended. The gift is one's life, and one's responsibility is to live it, otherwise one would not have been given it at all. Thistle's *From the Ashes* describes how he finds his truth through his experience with homelessness, drug addiction, and extensive physical, emotional, and psychological trauma. These experiences all lead him to a life he would never have realized had he not endured them. Frankl's purpose in *Man's Search for Meaning* was to survive his life's work and the love of his life during The Holocaust thus he too attests that there is meaning in suffering.

The more he listened, the more it was all around.

II

Story One

Born into a society driven by the allure of success and the fear of failure, her story was already written. The ancient Greeks had two different concepts of time, Kairos and Chronos. One can see time as Chronos—quantifiable, counting the seconds, minutes, hours, days, years, as the young woman did. A nine to five, paid for her time, unknowingly shackling herself to a clock, her day now scheduled around it.

7:00 AM—Wake up and start the coffee, make breakfast while it percolates.
7:15 AM—Eat breakfast.

7:30 AM—Shower, get dressed, and do your makeup.

8:00 AM—Drive to work.

9:00 AM—Arrive at the office and check emails.

9:30 AM—Give staff daily briefing: tasks to accomplish, and updates on projects.

10:00 AM—Meet with the boss to go over the company's weekly agenda and progress reports.

11:00 AM—Office tasks and personal work time.

12:30 PM—Lunch

1:00 PM—Out on the floor assisting and supervising employees.

2:00 PM—Check emails and additional personal work time.

3:00 PM—Meet with the boss to review the day's progress and discuss tasks for the next day.

4:00 PM—Compile discussion notes and data to create a task sheet for employees the next day.

5:00 PM—Grab a snack and exercise.

6:15 PM—Drive home.

7:15 PM—Shower.

7:30 PM—Make and eat dinner.

9:00 PM—Get ready for bed.

9:30 PM—Lights out.

In the Pocket

Of course, this was all fantasy land, for nothing ever goes according to plan. Her boss was inconceivably indecisive. Their meetings never ended on the hour and seemed to drag on for days at a time, issues never resolved until the last minute. For her, what needed to be done and how to go about doing it was black and white. For him, he valued input and mulled over her suggestions, sawing back and forth before choosing to do what he had always wanted to do in the first place, she assumed. She felt that his discussions about her ideas were lip service, and ultimately, a proverbial slap in the face. *What a waste of my time and the company's money,* she thought.

She had a vision and a goal to run her own company and believed that she could run it a lot more efficiently than the man she worked for now. The fact that he was an emerging business "guru" and the company was profitable, despite his "wastefulness", was an anomaly to her. It fed her frustrations and motivated her to prove she could do it better than him.

He said that running a business was an art, and that he acted based on the "feel" of each situation. He often made the right call under the highest moments of pressure. She failed to observe and listen, blinded by her ambition and passion. She believed that all she had to do was pay her dues, do her time under this façade of a CEO, and she would eventually be presented with her opportunity to climb the ladder.

Show me the answers and I will repeat them back to you.
Give me the law and I will follow.
Present the reason and I will be freed.

You see, her parents were successful, at least in the societal sense, and thus, she was born into expectation. If she wanted to make her parents proud, she would either have to match or exceed their financial successes and social status. The path, of course, started with school. To get a high paying job, you need a high paying education, and to get a high paying education, you need perfect marks—and a bit of money—which her parents had.

Repeat after me: "ABC, 123, now I know what teacher needs!" And, just like that, she was off to some preppy east coast university, indebted yet again to mom and dad's expectations. Flash forward through the memorization of more elaborate

In the Pocket

Dr. Seuss, and she was now second hand to a mockery of a CEO at one of the largest global companies.

As her boss's filibusters continued through the weeks, her daily tasks were pushed further into her evenings, and soon were consuming her mind. The worry of completing things on time, and the stress of not knowing her boss's intended next steps with the company, crept into her sleep. The company hummed along at a steady pace. As she lay awake most nights with her eyes shut, rumination and the cyclical fear of failure took turns on a never-ending Ferris wheel.

While the blueish tinge darkened under her eyes, and the bones of her skeleton sharpened in appearance, poking through her skin, the mogul, pleased with his prodigy's development over the years, presented her the opportunity of a lifetime: the proposal of a large merger with another re-nowned company in the industry. An opportunity to make each company billions if a partnership was agreed upon. He wanted to give her this experience to expand her knowledge for the eventual benefit of her own company one day. This spurred some much-needed enthusiasm within herself and reinvigorated her passion for her work. It also added more stress to her plate, but she obliged anyways—how could she not?

For months she crunched the numbers, combed the books, collected the data, and pieced together a portfolio. There was no oversight or guidance from the boss, just the task and a due date; the perfect scenario for her time management, competency, and efficiency skills to shine without obstruction. She was about to present perfection— every fine detail laid out, making it impossible to refute the evidence that both companies needed each other. Her eyes twinkled in the incandescence of her laptop as she scrolled over her completed body of work. The night before the presentation, she slept as good as ever, thinking about a job well done.

As she entered the sleepy-eyed room of suits, excited and a little nervous, she slowly handed out the three-inch thick manilla stacks of her time and effort to each executive. She slipped a small grin to her boss and quietly made her way back to the front of the room. Her boss noticed only the accountants attempting to flip past the first page, while the others craned their eyes from the text in front of them to the young woman at the front of the room. Then, the boss watched their eyes drift away from the young woman. Their heads started to bob, and their shoulders started to slouch, as she dove into the complexities of the merger. Even the accountants were less perky than before, turning their heads back to the numbers on the pages to find solace. After the executives had frequented their watches, and then the clock on the wall for comparison, the boss had observed their body language long enough and nudged his way into the presentation.

"Look it Jack, we've clearly done our homework on this merger and think it's the best option for both companies. I remember when..." And then he went on to tell some long story of how Jack's great great great twice removed grandfather went to war and fought alongside his ancestors in a great victory of some sort, much like the two CEOs were about to do right now. Everyone in the room was now erect, almost standing out of their seats, eyes bulging with intense desire to read the boss's lips as they dropped luscious words—even the accountants. All but one in the room was horned up by this exotic anecdote. The young woman receded to the deepest corner of the room with mixed emotions of shock, anger, and self-pity. She would not remember the boss's speech, for she was too flustered by his betrayal of her desires to listen.

After the deal was closed, everyone shook hands and beamed at the thought of scotch and cigars in celebration that night. With the success of the merger, the boss was much too ignorant to recognize what he had done to his finest pupil. He had undermined her presentation and had broken her trust. He gave some small tidbits on how to recapture an audience when presentations go awry, but his failure to understand who she was, and what this meant to her, deafened her ears; rage had encapsulated her ability to listen. *If he would've just let me finish, I would've landed the deal,* she thought, convinced even more now than before that she was ready for the next step.

After the merger, she no longer entertained his discussions, keeping her ideas concealed under the consensus that they would never be used. She tuned out his daily "squabble" and limited the likelihood of bumping into him at work outside of their meetings. Spent by her years of service to the company, and the lack of acknowledgement from her boss, she had reached her limits. Her 5:00 PM exercise became repeatedly picking up the bottle and putting it back down again.

In the Pocket

The company continued to succeed in its mysterious ways. With its success, and her long tenure, she had finally paid her dues, realizing the long-forgotten dream of running her own company. Not too long after taking over, the stress came back, and the worry once more prevented her from getting a good night's rest. She always thought she had all the answers, but she didn't. The things she said to employees seemed to go in one ear and out the other. When she explained what she thought to be simple concepts, they were met with confusion. And when other people presented ideas, she only thought them to be "right" or "wrong." Her frustrations set in, like before, at all the "incompetence" within her company. When errors and mistakes happened at the hands of her workers, she berated them. Worse, when these same mistakes were repeated after she explicitly explained them, she accused her workers of voluntarily disrespecting her authority. She suspected this disrespect was a result of her lack of experience, or the fact that she was a woman.

The newer workers succumbed to her increasingly frequent scare tactics and took extra care in doing everything exactly as she said. They were surprisingly her worst workers, producing little results compared to the "defiant" ones. The older workers found her scare tactics quite laughable. They'd do their best impressions after work at the local pub, soaking in gallons of cold beer and getting a jolt of relief from the camaraderie. Sometimes, they'd play games with her at work, poking the bear for a reaction. She caught onto their schemes and brought them in one by one, infuriated. She pounded her fists on the desk and screamed in maniacal elation that she "had been right all along," that they were "indeed voluntarily disrespecting her!" One by one, she dismissed them all, and was left only with the newcomers. *Perfect,* she thought. *I can shape them into the greatest workers, and my company can finally reach the prosperity it deserves.*

The company crumbled. Without any experienced workers, even the greatest editions of her training manuals couldn't create the production she needed to sustain her dream. As the sale of her company completed, her alcohol consumption increased. She was desperate to calm her mind and get some sleep. Even with the company and all its incompetent employees gone, the ire within her soul raged on. Every day there was something to be bitter about, and the more she drank, the more furious she became. She thought about how she used to have friends and loved ones. Whatever happened to them? Where did they disappear to? This made her sad, another reason to drink.

When the word got out that his once budding prodigy had fallen into the depths of suffering and despair, the boss called her up. She cursed him for not teaching her how to run her own company. Years later when he called up her parents, and they asked why he did not help her, he said, "I tried to tell her, but she wouldn't listen."

III

Story Two

Born into a society uprooted by exploitation and oppression that once lived in harmony with the earth and its creator, his story was already written. Driven by the wonderous forces of nature, he could never find his place in it, for his teachers weren't there. As the ancient Greeks would describe it, his time was spent qualitatively, through Kairos, rather than Chronos, shackled to his instincts, much like the bird that awoke him.

It sat perched on his open window shifting glances between the disheveled young man and the blue sky. It must have mistaken him for the roots of a tree since, only a moment ago, it had waded through his belongings sprawled along the floor scavenging for food and nesting materials, as if the young man's room were the forest. Only after the roots moved did the bird retreat to the window, now shifting glances curiously at this thing it couldn't quite make out. When the bird began to call out to friends to help in identifying this object, the young man stirred, peering at the bird to observe it. The bird's eyes fixed on the object moving towards it. As the young man reached out his hand, offering a root for the bird to climb onto, it took off in a flash. He shook his head with disappointment. He'd been unable to make a connection.

Now standing at the window, the young man observed the sun, the sky, the ocean, and then the street below. "What kind of day is it going to be?" he pondered. "Will it be too windy for the fishermen to go out? Is it going to rain later and cut their day short?" He loved the days when he awoke to a grey cloak of fog covering everything but the street below. This was the sign of a good day with clear skies, for when the sun was at its highest, the cloak would unveil its wonders.

It was the transition between dry season and wet season and as so, the weather was at its peak of unpredictability. It could feel like the heat would suffocate or the rain would flood.

He turned his attention to the streets below in search of foreigners. Each person that walked by, he examined closely. The color of their skin, the language they spoke, if they were in groups or alone, who perused from shop-to-shop zigzagging along the street, and who walked in a straight line at an even pace. He was broken from his morning trance by the sound of his stomach growling.

He made his way to the kitchen where his mother had instinctively started cooking breakfast. He grimaced at the sight of her ragged clothes, and her hard plastic sandals supported with wraps of duct tape.

"What's on for work today?" She peered at him over her shoulder.

"I'm not sure," he stated. "I might make my way down to the port to see if any captains need a hand. Looks like it's going to be a good day for fishing; the water is calm, and the sky is clear."

"I think you're onto something." She beamed, and served him the eggs she had borrowed from the neighbors.

He gazed at the plate in front of him, unfulfilled. Not wanting to upset her, he began to eat without looking up to avoid exposing his disappointment.

"You know," she continued. "I had a dream last night that you not just captained but owned your own ship! Your boat was always loaded with the finest of fish on your day's return, and people lined up at the port for stretches to pay top dollar for your catch. You had this sense of when to go out and when to stay in. Even on the clearest of days, when the water stood still, you sometimes chose to stay in. And on these days, when you chose to stay in, many who chose to go out either came back with their boats empty, or worse, suffered the perils of the wind and the rain."

The young man shook his head and laughed. "Maybe I will be the captain of my own ship one day." He smiled. "But if I am, I will only go out when the skies are clear, and the water is still. Or when the land is cloaked in grey in the morning. And I will only stay in when the perils of the wind and the rain are at my window."

"Ei yai yai, what am I going to do with you, my child!" She too shook her head and laughed while washing his empty plate.

He stood up and headed back to his bedroom to gather his belongings for the day's work, not noticing his stomach now quiet.

"You never listen," his mother said, smiling. She hugged him and kissed his forehead, before shoeing him out the door. She watched his feet as they disappeared into the distance, and then prepared for her own day's work in the market, ignoring her stomach still grumbling.

The young man scurried through town, and upon hearing rumblings of a large cruise ship set to dock the next day, he made his decision to work the market upon its arrival. At the port, he located a captain he worked for on occasion and asked if he needed work for the day. The captain obliged and stated that today was going to be a good day. "Plenty of fish out there to be brought home. I could use the extra hands." Elated by this, the young man eagerly prepped the boat.

They drifted along quite a while without seeing a trace of life, collecting only stray driftwood and seaweed. The captain remained calm and listened to the breeze, feeling the boat rock gently. The young man grew impatient and tried to hide his deepening frustration. The captain looked over him thoughtfully and then back out to sea. "Ahh yes," he exclaimed and pointed out in the distance. The young man followed the finger and strained his eyes, squinting against the sun to see. It was a bird scanning the ocean's surface.

The captain steered the ship and tailed the bird, matching its speed as it thrust its wings harder. The young man now saw what the bird and the captain saw—their friends circling and diving. As the boat drew closer, finned companions on the left and right dipped and dived, bottling towards the commotion, the deep blue water streaming along their sleek charcoal grey skin. The ball thrashed and sprayed as the school of fish frantically flopped to the surface to avoid the clutches from below and jumped into the clutches from above. The fishermen casted their lines to cash in their fill, the electricity of the chaos driving their insatiable pace. And just like that, as quickly as it started, the chaos now dissipated, sucked back into the deep blue.

As the orange sunk and the pinks, reds, and purples painted the sky, the fishermen returned. Three fish for their day's work. The captain handed the young man one of the fish and half a day's wages. The young man peered, heartbroken, at the change in his hand, and his shoulder nearly slunk out of its socket with sadness when he turned to drag the measly fish back home.

The captain put his hand on the young man's shoulder hoping to lift it back into place. "I know today was a tough one. I'd like for you to come back tomorrow; I have a feeling it's going to be a good day."

The young man said he would think about it, but he had already made up his mind before the day had begun, and with his hands now full of the day's disappointments, he confirmed his plans to work the market the next day.

His stomach growled again as he made his way home. When he entered the house, he sheepishly handed his mother the change and offered the fish for her to cook. She greeted him, beaming with open arms, and graciously accepted his offerings. "All in a single day's work!" She gleamed proudly and kissed her son on the forehead, thankful for her life's blessing.

She cooked the fish, along with the vegetables she was given at the market, set to spoil by day's end. He again sat and ate with hidden shame as his mother spun another web, this time about the marketplace.

In the Pocket

"I always imagined you'd be a great vendor one day, running your own shop. You'd import products of the highest quality, knowing the right amount to buy, and how to sell them too. You'd have the best margins out of all the vendors, and they'd clamor for advice from you. You'd hire the right workers and you'd know which areas of town to send them. But you wouldn't just know where to send them, you'd know when. You'd know at what period of the day, during which season, which specific worker would be sent to what area."

He smiled at the childlike whimsy of his mother.

"Maybe I will be the owner of a shop one day," he entertained her. "But I will only send the workers to the port that know how to speak English, and I will only send them on the days that large cruises arrive. I will keep the rest of them within the streets of the market and will not send them to other areas of town."

She folded her towel and swatted him playfully. "Must you never listen to my dreams for you, now wash your face and get to bed!" She giggled, her tired eyes growing heavy.

He smiled and adhered to her suggestion, peacefully falling asleep, his stomach quiet once again.

He woke up to the wind howling, and light drops of rain pecking his eyelids. He stared out the window at the white caps lining the ocean and thought of the foolish captain preparing to set sail for the day. After another discouraging pieced-together breakfast made by his mother, dressed in the same washed and pressed rags, he headed to the streets of the market looking for work.

He came across a familiar vendor that had done business with his mother. "Fancy seeing you around these parts. You must have heard of the large cruise ship coming into the port today. Look-ing for work?" The young man nodded. "Good, good! I'll tell you what, I heard the sun was going to poke its head through the clouds today and shine its brightest at the port, spotlighting all the foreigners as they exit the ship. Here is a display of the world's finest sunglasses, you can take it to the port and sell your heart's worth; you know how much those foreigners hate staring at the sun! Bring back the money from your sales at the end of the day and I'll give you your commission. Oh, and if you sell out, make your way back to me, and we'll pop the greatest bottle of champagne France has to offer! I might even hand you the keys to this shop myself!" And with a heavy thump on the back, the vendor sent the young man off to the port.

For the first while, he stayed in one place as the tourists glanced at his display and carried onward. He thought if he stayed in one spot with "the world's finest sunglasses", they would scan amongst the other displays in comparison and eventually come back to him desiring the pair they had first glanced at; if he moved, he would miss the opportunity for a sale upon their return. With his broken English, he tried to describe the wonderful qualities of his sunglasses, but this seemed to move the tourists away quicker than before. They'd sometimes chuckle and say, "No thank you," or make up some excuse like "I already have a pair." Some felt genuine pity for the young man and explained that they would've bought a pair had they the change on them. The young man stared hopelessly at the clouds the vendor had said would clear. *Maybe I'm not being persistent enough,* he thought.

He decided to change his strategy, now following tourists down the streets and along the beaches, to the point of begging, half in his own language, half in theirs, desperate for a sale. This only quickened their distance from him. As the sun pulled beneath the clouds, receding nearly below the horizon, he retreated to his vending spot where he had begun his day, next to the cruise ship prepared for departure.

Familiar faces from the day trudged past him, carrying bags full of souvenirs and gifts, their eyes not glancing at his display, his face unrecognizable to them. Off in the distance, he saw the captain unloading his haul from the day, people lining up endlessly to throw silver at his feet for a taste of his catch. The young man reached into his empty pockets and hung his head low with defeat. A young couple returning to the port squinted through the pink, purple, and red rays of the sunset, reminding them that they still needed to pick up a pair of sunglasses on their trip. The dreary day had caused them to forget this necessity, and at the moment the rays touched their minds, they saw the young man and his display.

They picked and probed, asking him questions about how he thought they looked wearing the different pairs. "Yeah, yeah! Good, good!" the young man would respond with his thumbs up, though their questions he hardly understood. He pulled out the makeshift mirror his vendor had provided him with and handed it to the couple. The couple smiled and laughed, accepting the kind gesture of a broken car mirror taped to a comb. They took turns ogling and exchanging looks, like a hairdresser would after finishing a haircut. "Ooo! Ahhh!" the couple played humorously. Even the young man couldn't help but laugh and join in on the fun, taking the mirror and showing them off to each other. After the couple bought their sunglasses, they skipped gleefully back to the ship, and the young man watched them cheerfully before packing up his display and returning to the vendor.

His cheerfulness was soon washed away by the small change in his pocket. He arrived back at the shop, returning the display, the silver from his two sales, and the handy mirror. The vendor, as promised, gave the young man his cut of the sales. The weight of the change in his hand felt less than yesterday's. A tear began to well in his eye, and dropped shamefully before he had the chance to turn around and leave.

"Tough day, I see," said the vendor solemnly.

"Yes," said the young man. "The sun never came," he quipped. He picked up his head to look at the vendor's expression.

The vendor smiled. "My boy," he proceeded, "the sun rises and sets every day, and someone will always need a pair of sunglasses." He pointed to the change in the young man's hand. "Come back tomorrow and I will show you how to sell. What an amazing start you have made today!" The young man said he would think about coming back to the vendor, but he remembered the weight of the change from yesterday, and the captain's haul today, and had already made his decision to go back to the captain for work tomorrow.

When he returned home dinner was nearly ready. His mother rushed to the door and kissed him on the forehead twice. "Oh, my child how I was nearly sick that you hadn't returned yet!"

"Yes, I'm sorry, I was late returning from the port."

"Ah, of course, busy making sales, I should've known!" she bubbled; her hysteria now subsided.

"Not really." He admitted as he reached into his pocket and placed the change carelessly on the table.

In the Pocket

She put her hands on her hips and shook her head. "You made your way back to me safely, *and* you have offerings to give!? Come sit and enjoy this wonderful meal with me. The neighbors lost a chicken today to the terrors of the night and gave it to us. Since it was not slaughtered in a clean manner, it would not have been viable to sell at the market. How blessed we are, the creator always protects us if we listen."

The next morning his friend was back to wake him, this time pecking at his arm. He swatted at the bird to make it go away, but this only stirred a frenzy within his room, the two flinging their belongings in all directions. Only when his mother opened the door did order restore. The bird flew out the window, and her son sat in a heap, flabbergasted. She laughed heartily at the scene and told him to get dressed and come out for breakfast.

He scampered to the window after she shut the door, hoping to catch the culprit responsible for the disaster in his room. The bird was nowhere to be seen, and his attention soon drew to the landscape cloaked in grey. *A Fisherman's Dream!* he thought. Hastily, he scrounged together his belongings and sprinted out the door.

"Don't you want breakfast?" his mother shouted.

"Can't, Fisherman's Dream!" he hollered back.

She gazed gleefully at his trail of dust left behind.

By the time he reached the port, the fog was starting to clear. He scanned ecstatically for the captain, in what seemed like the longest moment of his life. Eventually, he spotted him preparing the boat to set sail. He ran to the captain, fearful that he would leave without him on this glorious day.

"I knew you'd come back." The captain winked with a smile. "Today is going to be a good day," he proclaimed, as the two fishermen pushed off into the clear skies and still water.

They drifted through time without a bird in sight, or sleek charcoal grey fin to guide them. Not even the driftwood nor the seaweed welcomed their boat. As the sun set, the young man's stomach was now screaming. The captain casted a trawl net for the ride home in hopes that he could feed the young man for his troubles. The net scraped up a couple of oysters from the ocean's floor, and the captain happily placed them in the young man's hands, along with a quarter day's wages. He scoffed at the captain's offerings but took them anyway.

"Yes," the captain concurred. "Today has been a tough day, but it will come back to us. The creator is testing our will. Please, come back tomorrow and I will show you the creator's truth."

"And why would I come back to fish with you when the weight of my change is less than the day's prior, and the food for which I came is scarcer than before?"

The captain shook his head and chuckled. "Aye, the food is scarcer than before, and the weight of the change less, but even still, you have food to eat, and change to bring back to your mother. And the fish only live in the sea. Come back tomorrow and I will show you how to fish." The young man wanted to throw the captain's offerings into the ocean from which they came in response, but instead lied, saying he'd think about coming back to the captain. He had already made his decision that he would go back to the vendor, where his commissions had weighed heavier.

On his way home, the young man could not bear the noise of his stomach any longer, and smashed the oysters upon a rock, slurping their insides. Still, after the mass carnage, his stomach continued to scream. He thought of his mother's patched rags and her scanty, pieced-together meals and wept uncontrollably. His tears swept through anger and shame as he felt the light weight of the change in his pocket. *It's more useful spent than saved,* he thought. Drawn into the lights and gleeful shouts of a local bar, he searched for anything to soothe his pain. Before entering the establishment, he peered into the window of the vendor's shop. The world's finest sunglasses display was empty, a "Sold Out" sign hanging over it. The young man sank in hopelessness.

He stumbled home, pockets no longer weighted. His mother rushed to the door, the same way he had rushed out that morning, and caught her limp child in her arms. She stroked his hair and kissed his forehead in between gut-wrenching sobs, carried him to bed, and tucked him in. "Rest easy my child," she said with another kiss, and closed the door. She did not sleep that night, her stomach screaming in anguish. The creator had sacrificed her meal for the protection of her son. She was grateful for this.

And so it went for some time, the young man looking out his bedroom window every morning, judging the sun, the sky, the ocean, and the streets before choosing a path for that day. His life seemed inescapable. Only through the drink did he find relief. Each day, he always found a way to make enough for the habit, while still offering a small portion of his earnings to his mother. She continued to save every coin, no matter how small, and counted her blessings. She kissed her child when he left the house in the morning and caught him when he stumbled through the door at night.

Eventually she saved enough to buy him a small fishing boat and some gear. Elated by the sight of the boat docked at the port, the young man envisioned the type of captain he would be. He would be smarter than the rest, only going out when the weather was pleasant. It was now his responsibility to maintain the boat and catch the fish.

With his days at sea limited to when the weather was agreeable, and the lack of fish caught on these days, he struggled to break even. His renewed vigor for life was soon extinguished and his drinking habit worsened. He sold almost all his fishing gear to maintain his addiction. And now, when he came across a valuable thrashing and spraying bait ball, he did not have the proper gear to reap the rewards. Exhausted by his life of poverty, and the temporary relief alcohol provided, he fell to his knees one night and begged the creator to end his suffering.

The next morning the young man awoke half remembering what he had asked for and looked out his window. There it was. The dark grey cloak. The creator had answered his call for help. He sprinted to the port and arranged what little gear he had in preparation for the Fisherman's Dream.

The captain, seeing this, walked over to the young man with a grave look on his face. "Today is not a good day," he said quietly to the young man, his head hanging low.

The young man paused and looked at the captain smiling. "No, my captain, today is a good day. You see, I asked the creator to relieve me of my suffering and he has given me the Fisherman's Dream."

The captain shook his head. "Do you not remember what happened to us the last time we went out fishing together on a day like today? Do you not remember what happened *to you* on that day? No, my boy, today is not a good day. If you set sail, you will never return."

The young man laughed in disbelief. "You have set sail on countless days worse than this and yet you still breathe today, telling another captain how to man their ship, no less!"

"Aye, it is because I learned to fish from another captain that I stand here today. I have lived this sea long enough to know when not to."

The young man furiously undid his last knot at the captain's last plea and pushed off before the fog began to dissipate. It never did, and the young man never returned.

His mother ran to the port the next morning only to find the captain motionless staring at the horizon. "I told the boy, but he wouldn't listen," he confirmed.

She wept into the waves, for she always knew her child was a part of the circle of life. The bird from the young man's room flew past their mother's tears and landed on the shoreline, wading through to pick up debris for its nest and food for its newborn.

IV

Some Insights from Story Three

Born into a life experience unique to him, the man was driven to understand what it all meant. He knew he had to create structure within the spontaneity of life to help guide his purpose. Like the shepherd in *The Alchemist,* he had to achieve his "personal legend": He had to follow the signs of his life, and they would lead him to his purpose (Coelho 24). That is why the creator created him. And what that purpose was, he already knew. It was his intuition, his gut feelings. But if he only followed his instincts, they would mislead him down the wrong path. You see, animals only follow their instincts, and what separated the two was the mind that the creator gifted the man. A mind of reasoning.

An animal's instinct is to fight, flee, or freeze in the face of danger since these actions might save their life. Likewise, its behaviors are guided by the search for food and shelter to survive. And because the man had these instincts as well, he too was biologically wired to seek safety in the face of danger. But, as Maurer speaks of, the man's life was rarely ever in danger as his body still perceived (42-43). And because of his mind's ability to reason, he knew better than to always avoid uncomfortable situations in his life. In fact, it was because of this ability to reason that the man could distinguish between an actual threat and a perceived threat, and harnessing this was the key to his treasure. He had to act in accordance with his soul in the face of adversity.

In opposition to the purpose of an animal to simply survive, if the man ignored his instincts and tried to force his path solely through logic and reasoning, he would never hit his intended target. He had to listen to his thoughts, and his emotions tied to his personal experiences. Let it be clear that personal experiences are not always related to oneself; they often involve the observations of and interactions with others.

Anyways, back to his story. He knew his structure had to involve both concepts of time, Kairos *and* Chronos. That is, he didn't want to spend too much quantifiable amount of qualitative time in one area without allocating enough for another. With this idea, he made a small to-do list of no more than three things each day that would get him closer to actualizing his purpose. In this way, he would be able to devote enough quality time to each task without the worry that life's spontaneity would interfere with its completion. Moreover, he could now devote more quality time to life's spontaneity because he had a manageable number of tasks to complete each day.

Since he formulated his to-do list in accordance with his purpose, he was passionate about what he did each day. And because he was passionate about what he did each day, he wanted to do it thoroughly to the best of his ability. And when he did these things to the best of his ability, measurable time became irrelevant. He was immersed in each task and could work without the urge to eat or sleep. The only thing he wanted to do was keep doing what he was doing. *Yes,* he thought. *Do*

In the Pocket

three things you're passionate about a day, and the sun's length in the sky will be long enough to achieve them. When he did his three things a day, freeing up time to listen to life's spontaneity, he saw patterns that corresponded to his tasks; what he learned in life's curious moments guided the tasks he did each day. Everything was related and had been driving him towards his purpose all along, just as Coehlo had written (24). The hard moments became easier to navigate when he chose to solve them, rather than hide from them. His clarity was an addiction.

V

Story Three Continued

When he thought back on his journey, it really was a search for companionship that led the man to where he was now. He wanted to find someone who understood the way he thought; someone who empathized with his life experiences. Someone who shared his ideas of life and what it meant to live happily. He never felt comfortable being who he was, so he never could connect with someone like him. He knew that someone was out there, but, with time, his faith wavered. All the people he met were nice, yet his gut would tell him no. Each time his gut would tell him no, he would relay its message to the people, and he would drink away his sorrow and loneliness.

He hated his work and dreaded the days, staring at the hands of the clock to relieve him of his misery. The weekends were even worse, short staffed and working overtime. His co-workers were nice enough, and supported him through the hard moments, which seemed to be more often now. Staff morale began to sag as layoffs increased with the shutdowns of outdated departments. With the increased layoffs came an increased workload, and a lack of compensation. His co-workers left one by one of their own accord and gave him their duties to carry. There was no relief from the mess, and he had vivid nightmares every time he laid down to sleep.

He couldn't afford to drink his woes, for the next day hangover would impair the sharpness required to get all his work done on time, so he refrained from drinking on the nights before. He had to find a different outlet. The contemplation of quitting, and the fear of hanging his co-workers out to dry, were rapidly sprouting in his head. He decided to discuss his concerns with his boss. She validated his feelings and provided him with a prayer that stuck with him.

God, grant me the serenity to accept the things I cannot change,
The courage to change the things I can,
And the wisdom to know the difference.

This seemed to calm his mind, and he recited it often in his head during times of distress. Still, the ever-growing hatred for his work overcame any new coping mechanism he tried. His co-workers bickered more about the overriding bureaucracy within the department, and a few weeks later, after more responsibilities had been stripped from him and allocated to upper management with higher professional credentials, he put in his transfer request. As much as it hurt him, he knew it was time. His boss, who had hired him, and who had consoled him in his times of need, was being pushed out the door. And the co-workers who he had started with were now scarce in number.

His transfer was short lived. He became unhappy once again with his work only two months into the new position. The hours were better, he had more personal office time, he got the weekends off, and his pay increased, yet none of it mattered. He needed to do what he loved. Though he had to swallow the large sum he had paid for an education to follow a career path he no longer wanted to pursue, he gave his two weeks' notice. And he was now on the hunt for a job he was passionate about, with enough cash to cover only two months' rent. Two weeks before his two months were up, and fifteen interviews later, he was offered the job of his dreams. It was a significant pay cut from the one before, but he didn't care. He was happy to be making money doing something he loved.

With no professional experience in the field, he entered an entry level position, and was quite nervous about his qualifications. Ironically, without his degree from an accredited post-secondary institution, he wouldn't have met the minimum requirements for the application. *Not a waste of money after all,* he thought. He remembered his boss stating in the interview "I don't care about your experience or expertise; we can work on that. All I care about is that I can trust you." Guided by his compass of loyalty, the man forever committed to doing his best for the person who gave him the chance to live out his dream. His work ethic, dedication, and service developed the trusting relationship his boss had asked for.

The two of them—boss and co-corker—came to understand and appreciate the full picture of who the other person was, and why each of them did the things they did. In this way, they fed off each other and created a dream team, free of any weaknesses. Yet, it was not always easy in the beginning. The man wanted to do it all at once, and the boss had to step in and pull the reins when the man got carried away. This frustrated the man, eager to prove himself. In these moments, the man reminded himself of his lack of expertise, and trusted that the boss knew what he was doing. The man sat back and observed.

He admired his boss's patience, and his ability to find solutions seemingly on instinct. However, there was nothing patient about his boss's approach to resolving a problem once he found it— he attacked it instantly. And when he resolved the problem, it never resulted in conflict. The boss had a unique way of making someone feel at ease, as he simultaneously crucified them. Employees left his office almost happier than when they came. The boss never accused or pointed the finger. He'd say in a calm manner, "This is how your actions are being perceived throughout the company. Can you see how other people may think that your intentions are ill-willed?" The employee would provide an explanation for their actions, and the two would solve the problem together.

Another uniqueness his boss possessed was that he never demanded things. This was something the man had to get used to. He showed up on the first day not knowing what to do in his newly furnished office. His boss did not bark orders. Instead, he discussed small things, seemingly trivial at the time; he briefed the man on housekeeping matters, daily ongoings of employees, small nuances and patterns beginning to emerge, and a vague direction the company needed to go. Thus, the man had to use his best judgement for the use of his time. He started with the small, tangible, housekeeping items. The boss took notice of the man's attentiveness to the little things, and once he felt it was time, the boss gave the man a little more responsibility. Through this process, the man learned the whole scope of the company to the smallest detail.

With this knowledge of the company's operations, the man could locate weaknesses within its structure and cultivate the next steps to progress it further. Their trust was built so strongly, and he knew his boss's thoughts so well, that their visions of the company were eventually unified. The man no longer needed to ask if he was on the right path, or doing the right things, because he knew what he wanted was now the same as what the boss wanted. What started as a desire to climb the ladder became less important the longer he worked alongside the boss, and the man realized that he was vicariously managing the company simply by doing his best for the one he worked for.

In the beginning, he would observe and imitate the boss. His mannerisms, the way he spoke, how he handled situations. The man thought to be like a great, he had to act like a great. But he did not get the results he desired. It wasn't until he started to ask the boss why he did the things he did, that the man realized that his answers would never be his boss's answers. In response to the man's questions, the boss responded, "I don't even remember what I do half the time, I just go with my gut and make it sound like I know what I'm doing." This response shifted the man's perspective. Now whenever the boss pulled the reins on him, the man would listen to the boss's critiques, and then choose which ones might work for him in the future. If imitating his boss did not work, and being himself was still insufficient because of his lack of experience, he would have to find a common ground, using some pieces of his boss's advice while still adhering to his values, to develop his own leadership style. He continued to grow professionally and was at peace knowing he was learning something new every day.

VI

Conclusion

When the man made his vow to give his very best every day to his boss, he never envisioned it would lead him to give up drinking. With the responsibility of helping a company succeed, and the uncertainty of when a task might need to be completed, he was always on call and had to stay sharp. After he stopped drinking it felt like a fog had been lifted. His thoughts were clearer, his senses more acute. His food smelled and tasted better. His dreams were more vivid. But when he went on a vacation, surrounded by family and friends, there was an expectation that he would drink with them in celebration, and he didn't have an excuse not to. The ebbs and flows of holiday binges, followed by weeks of sobriety on the job, magnified the stark differences between the two states.

When he was drunk with his friends and family, it was a whirlwind of laughs and happiness. He'd drink himself to sleep, the world going dark for a couple of hours. Then, he would wake up with his tongue caked dry from mouth breathing. His mind would rifle through anxious thoughts as the sun peaked on the horizon. "Where am I? What time is it? Where is my stuff?" When he had all the answers to his questions, he would get up, pacing around the house for something to do. He usually went for a run in these instances, in hopes that anxieties would seep out of his body along with the sweat. He'd return to the house afterwards and devour food, oddly hungrier than usual, while waiting for others to stir.

He suddenly had so much to discuss on these days, relaying his recollections from the night. His mind blabbered frantically, flipping from thought to thought and repeating sentences to make sure he didn't forget to say them. He couldn't remember a time when he had been so interested in having a conversation. His body was jittery and alternated between hot and cold sweats to eliminate the alcohol. It was usually around late afternoon when the crash began to settle in. At this point, he had to choose whether to quit while he was ahead or extend the eventual completion of the hangover. He always chose the latter, perking up after his first drink—back in the saddle. It was like he had hit the reboot button and was back up and running, good to go.

As the cycle repeated day in and day out, his body continued to function in disarray. He sometimes went for a week without a bowel movement. He didn't crave food after the first drink of the day. His memory was a blur, not knowing what happened on which day, and not remembering the conversations he was apparently so interested in having at the time. And his emotions were completely out of his control, bawling like a toddler—distraught that his friend had to leave, that same friend he had screamed at a minute ago.

It took him three days after his last drink to feel his senses again.

In his long stints of sobriety, his mind could once again flourish. Yet there was always a moment at the day's end, when his work was complete, that his longing for companionship returned.

In the Pocket

Since he had to refrain from drinking in these moments, he turned to other distractions. Television and food were his comforts. He would warm his soul through these vices until he grew tired and weary enough to fall asleep. Finally, the day came when he met her.

It was at a family wedding, the man back in his drunken craze. The conversationalist from within was evoked and he latched on to her. She too carried the conversation with equal interest. The two talked through the night until dawn without feeling the urge to sleep, quantifiable time not a concept, as they immersed themselves in each other. He, for once, would remember this one.

She was smart and intuitive, knowing the things she wanted to do, and the things she was passionate about. She did not force them into existence. She toiled with these ideas about her life's work, and what it meant to do something she loved, all the while understanding that it took concentrated time and effort to accomplish something. She was whimsical in a beautiful way. A childlike curiosity with a sophisticated understanding of the world around her.

She validated the life experiences and feelings he shared with her, never judging, always listening. She simply lent an ear, only providing her thoughts when she sensed he was seeking her guidance. She made him feel comfortable in being himself, and he was not afraid to share his secrets with her. She made him want to tell her every-thing, no matter how small, or how embarrassing, or how shameful. She accepted his insecurities.

They both agreed that people made things more complicated than they had to be. They agreed that life was easy—if nobody was dying, then everything would be alright.

With the comfort of finally connecting with someone in this world, his mind was freed to push forward towards his purpose. He could now use those moments at a day's end to grow where he needed to. He had an impulse to take care of his mind more, an obligation to be the best version of himself for her. The television he watched, the food he ate, the sleep he got, the exercise he did, it was all either pushing him closer to or further from what he needed to do to fulfill his obligation to her.

And so, his journey began.

He knew watching television was a mindless waste of time. His compromise was to watch something at least informative. Documentaries seemed to fit. Autobiographies, murder mysteries, conspiracies, underdog stories, all sparked his curiosity and made him think. But he soon again became unsatisfied. The films somehow always spun the narrative to make him believe the directors' intentions. There had to be a dramatic effect to keep the audience hooked. A story to be told and finished. A sort of bending of the truth to make him hear what they wanted him to hear. They always showed two sides of a story in a way that made him root only for one. His mind needed to be stimulated, not controlled, he thought.

But watching these movies was a difficult habit to kick, a form of relaxation and escape, equally as addictive as drinking. He had a plan. He would turn to reading, something that he wasn't interested in, but something certainly more stimulating than the brainwash he consumed now.

His grandmother would always ask, "Have you done any reading lately?"

And he would always respond, "No, not really. I do enough for school and work. It's not something I like to do in my spare time. I should read more though."

"Oh." She'd pause. "What do they have you reading in school?"

"Textbooks and research articles, nothing I really like to read."

"Well," she'd state, "it's a great way to stay sharp and pass the time." And then she'd go on to describe all the books she had been reading lately, which aunt, or uncle, or brother, or sister had gotten them for her, her opinions about the books, and her beliefs as to why each person picked the book to gift to her.

"I know I should read more, but I'm always so busy; I never have the time," he'd lie.

When he'd visit her again, she'd ask again, "So, what have you been reading lately?" Then she would showcase her stacks of books, picking up a few here and there to give her elevator pitch about why he might like to read them. "I have so many books that I don't know what to do with. Every time I turn around somebody's buying me a new one! Please sweets, help yourself, take some with you before you go," she'd plead.

"Yeah, I might." And he would politely take a couple before he left.

Now, the books collecting dust around his house had another purpose besides pleasing his grandmother. He told his soulmate of his plan to replace channels with chapters. "Every time I reach for the remote, I will pick up a book instead."

His word was his bond, but still, he struggled to pick up a book. Every day they would talk, and she would ask, "Did you read today?"

And he would have to admit his truth, and tell her, "No."

Like always, she never chastised him for his failure, and continued the conversation like nothing had changed from the moments before. And it was because of this subtle, nonthreatening question from her each day, much like his grandmother's gentle pushes to take her books, and his former boss's mention of *The Serenity Prayer*, that he finally picked up a book.

Had he not been comfortable sharing his truest wishes and vulnerabilities with his soulmate, he would have never picked up a book. And once he picked it up, he could never put it back down. And the more he read, the more things started to make sense. And the more things started to make sense, the more he wanted to share his truth. And the more he wanted to share his truth, the more he pondered the ways through which he could share it best. And the more he pondered the ways through which he could share it best, the more he drifted towards writing. And when he chose to write, he had to learn how. And when they told him to read, he compiled his list of the "greatest novellas of all time." And when he knocked off the books one by one, day by day, page by page, his ideas began to form. And when his ideas began to form, he wrote his first sentence. And when he wrote his first sentence, he wanted to write more. And when his ideas began to structure themselves on the pages, his truth was complete, and his purpose was actualized.

Isn't it funny how he strove for intellectual growth during his periods of sobriety yet craved human connection? And how he strove for human connection in his stints of drunkenness yet craved clarity and order? And how it was in his state of drunkenness that he met his soulmate, who, in turn, led him to achieve his life's purpose? There's a colloquialism people use to describe the perfect drunk. It is a feeling where you have had just enough liquor to experience its wonderous effects, maintaining your wits about you while ever so perfectly feeling the release of tension, without yet slipping into the perils of having too much. They call this being "in the pocket." He was in the pocket of life.

Works Cited

Coelho, Paulo, et al. *The Alchemist*. 25th anniversary edition. New York, NY, HarperOne, 2014.

Fisher, Carl Erik. *The Urge: Our History of Addiction*. New York, NY, Allen Lane, 2022.

Frankl, Victor E. 1907-1997. *Man's Search for Meaning: An Introduction to Logotherapy*. 4th ed. Boston, MA, Beacon Press, 1992.

Maurer, Robert. *One Small Step Can Change Your Life: The Kaizen Way*. New York, NY, Workman, 2014.

Thistle, Jesse. *From the Ashes*. New York, NY, Simon & Schuster, 2019.

www.ingramcontent.com/pod-product-compliance
Lightning Source LLC
Chambersburg PA
CBHW052026030426
42335CB00026B/3295